How do they work?

Puppets

Wendy Sadler

Heinemann Library
Chicago, Illinois

a division of Reed Elsevier Inc.
Chicago, Illinois

Customer Service 888-454-2279
Visit our website at www.heinemannlibrary.com

Editorial: Andrew Farrow and Dan Nunn
Design: Ron Kamen and Dave Oakley/Arnos Design
Picture Research: Hannah Taylor
Production: Duncan Gilbert

Originated by Ambassador Litho Ltd
Printed and bound in China by South China Printing Company.

09 08 07 06 05
10 9 8 7 6 5 4 3 2 1

Library of Congress Cataloging-in-Publication Data
Sadler, Wendy.
  Puppets / Wendy Sadler.
      p. cm. -- (How do they work?)
  Includes bibliographical references and index.
  ISBN 1-4034-7301-3 (library binding-hardcover) -- ISBN 1-4034-7302-1 (pbk.)
  1. Puppet making--Juvenile literature. 2. Puppets--Juvenile literature. I. Title.
  TT174.7.S23 2005
  791.5'3--dc22
                                    2004024040

Acknowledgements
The publishers would like to thank the following for permission to reproduce photographs:
Alamy Images pp. **18** (Mike Blenkinsop), **26** (Dave Pattison); Corbis pp. **5** (Julio Donoso), **14** (Jose Luis Pelaez Inc.), **15** (Werner Forman), **19** (Mitchell Gerber), **21** (Jim Sugar), **27** (John R. Jones/Papilio); Harcourt Education Ltd (Tudor Photography) pp. **4, 6, 7, 8, 9, 10, 11, 12, 13, 17, 22, 23, 28–29**; Pete Jones (ArenaPAL) p. **25**; Reuters (Jason Reed) p. **16**; Getty Images (Photodisc) p. **24**; Science Photo Library p. **20**.

Cover photograph reproduced with permission of Harcourt Education Ltd (Tudor Photography).

Contents

Some words are shown in bold, **like this**. You can find out
what they mean by looking in the glossary.

Puppets

A puppet is a **model** of a person or an animal. You can move puppets using your fingers, hands, strings, or **rods**.

4

Puppets come in lots of different shapes and sizes. You can make your own puppets at home. You can also see puppets on television!

Finger Puppets

A finger puppet is a small puppet that fits on your finger. You move the puppet by bending or moving your finger. You can even have five puppets on one hand!

Your fingers go in here.

Finger puppets can be made of **fabric** or **plastic**. In some finger puppets, your fingers become legs!

7

Hand Puppets

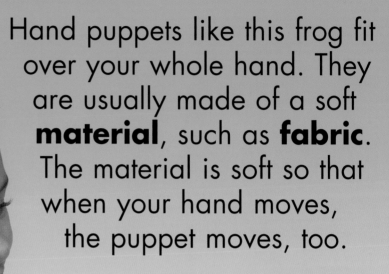

Hand puppets like this frog fit over your whole hand. They are usually made of a soft **material**, such as **fabric**. The material is soft so that when your hand moves, the puppet moves, too.

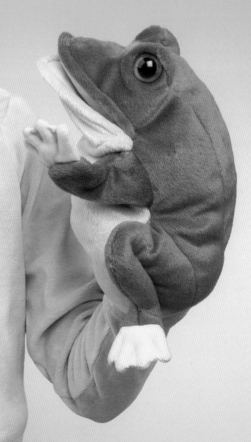

Your fingers go in here.

Your thumb goes in here.

You can make a hand puppet from a sock. Your thumb becomes the mouth of the puppet. Your fingers become the head. You can make the puppet "talk" by moving your fingers and thumb.

Puppets with Legs

With some hand puppets, your fingers become the legs. This puppet is a big insect. Your front two fingers become the insect's legs.

Your fingers go in here.

With this puppet all your fingers are used as legs. A spider has eight legs, but you have only four fingers and a thumb. Some of the puppet legs will not have a finger in them.

Puppets with Strings

You can make
this puppet move
without even
touching it!
You move it
by pulling on
the strings.

12

When you pull a
string tied to a leg,
you lift the leg. You
can make a string
puppet walk by
pulling the strings
in the right order.

Puppets on Rods

rods

Some puppets can be moved using **rods**. You push the rods to make different parts of the puppet move.

joints

rod

This rod puppet has **joints**. The joints let the arms move. Puppets with joints can be made to move, like real people and animals.

15

Puppet Materials

Different puppets are made of different **materials**. Puppets on **rods** need to be **stiff** so they can stand up. If they were made of soft material, they would just fall over!

strings

Puppets on strings are often made of wood. Wood is a stiff material. These puppets need to have **joints**.

wood

joint

Big Puppets

Some puppets are very big. They can be moved by a person inside the puppet. This monster puppet has a person inside. The person moves his or her arms to make the arms of the monster move.

This is Big Bird from the television show *Sesame Street*.

Some puppets have **controls** in their head. Pushing a button or pulling a **lever** makes the eyes or face move. Big Bird's eyes work like this.

19

Animatronics

Some puppets work using machines. They are called **animatronic** puppets. This is what the inside of an animatronic puppet looks like.

Animatronic puppets can look very real. These two animatronic animal puppets were made for a television show.

animatronic puppets

Shadow Puppets

Shadow puppets can be made of thick cardboard. The cardboard blocks a light shining on a wall. Where the light is blocked, a shadow forms that is the same shape as the cardboard.

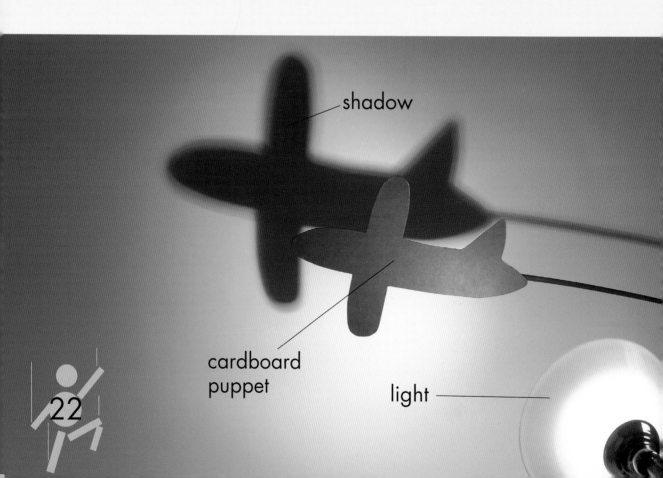

shadow

cardboard puppet

light

You also can make shadow puppets with your hands. The shadows will get bigger if you move your hands closer to the light.

Puppets That Glow in the Dark

Some puppets are made of special **materials**. These make the puppets glow in the dark when a special light shines on them.

People who move puppets often wear black clothes. This means they cannot be seen in the dark. The puppets seem to be moving by themselves, because you cannot see the people who are moving them.

Puppet Shows

These children are watching a puppet show. The puppets are moved by someone hiding inside the tall box.

String puppets need a **stage** with room above it for people to stand. This is so they can pull the strings to make the puppets move.

Put on Your Own Puppet Show

You can put on your own puppet shows by making a stage. These are some of the things you will need to do:

- Write a short story, or play, for your puppets to perform.
- Make puppets for each character in the play.
- Build a simple **stage** that can be put on a table.
- Practice your play.
- Invite people to come see your play.

Glossary

animatronic puppet that looks like a real animal or person. It is controlled by a machine.

controls buttons and levers that make something work

fabric soft material, such as cotton or wool

joint place where two moving things are joined together

lever simple machine that makes it easier to move something

material what something is made of

model copy of something else

plastic light material that can be made in many shapes and colors

rod long, thin pole

shadow dark shape made when something is between a surface and a bright light

stage part of a theater where the actors or puppets perform

stiff something that is hard to bend

More Books to Read

Burkholder, Kelly. *Puppets.* Vero Beach, Fl.: Rourke Publishing, 2000.

Kennedy, John. *Puppet Mania!* Cincinnati: North Light Books, 2004.

Smith, Thomasina. *Crafty Puppets.* Milwaukee: Gareth Stevens Publishing, 1999.

Wulffson, Don. *Toys! Amazing Stories Behind Some Great Inventions.* New York: Henry Holt and Co., 2000.

Index